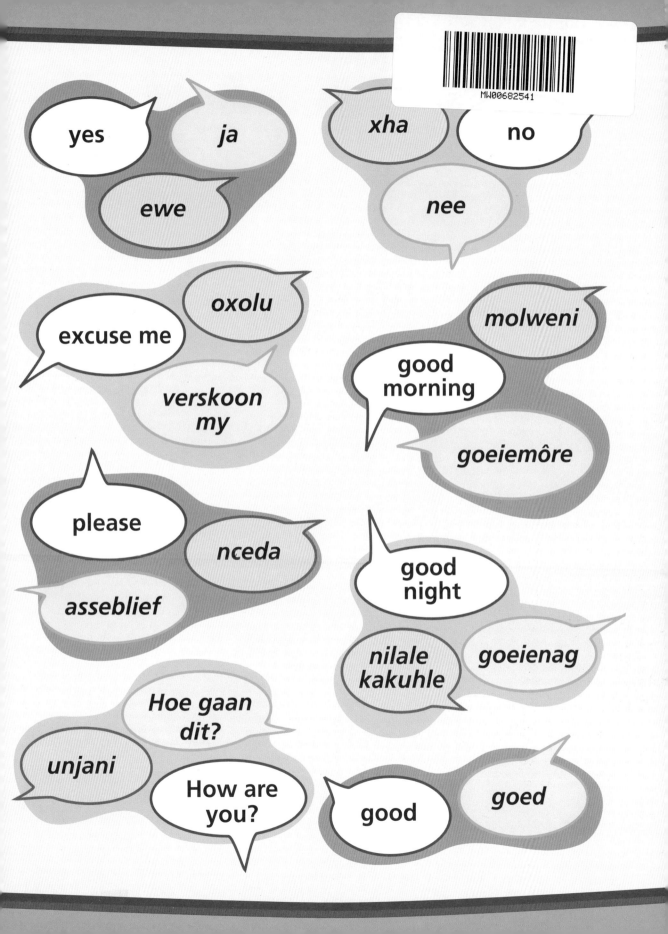

Welcome to South Africa

Meredith Costain   Paul Collins

This edition first published in 2002 in the United States of America by Chelsea House Publishers, a subsidiary of Haights Cross Communications

Chelsea House Publishers
1974 Sproul Road, Suite 400
Broomall, PA 19008–0914

The Chelsea House world wide web address is www.chelseahouse.com

Library of Congress Cataloging-in-Publication Data Applied for.
ISBN 0-7910-6540-5

First published in 2000 by
Macmillan Education Australia Pty Ltd
627 Chapel Street, South Yarra, Australia, 3141

Copyright © Meredith Costain and Paul Collins 2000

Edited by Miriana Dasovic
Text design and page layout by Goanna Graphics (Vic) Pty Ltd
Cover design by Goanna Graphics (Vic) Pty Ltd
Maps by Stephen Pascoe
Illustrations by Vaughan Duck
Printed in Hong Kong

Acknowledgements
The author and the publisher are grateful to the following for permission to reproduce copyright material:

Cover photograph: African masks at a craft market, Lonely Planet Images © Richard I'Anson.

Angela Costain pp. 27 (bottom), 30; Lonely Planet Images, pp. 7 (bottom), 11–13, 22, 23, 25, 26, 27 (top), 28, 29 © Richard I'Anson, pp. 19 (right), 21 © Andrew MacColl; Jon Murray pp. 5, 6, 7 (top), 8–10, 15, 18, 19 (left), 20, 24, 30.

While every care has been taken to trace and acknowledge copyright the publishers tender their apologies for any accidental infringement where copyright has proved untraceable.

Contents

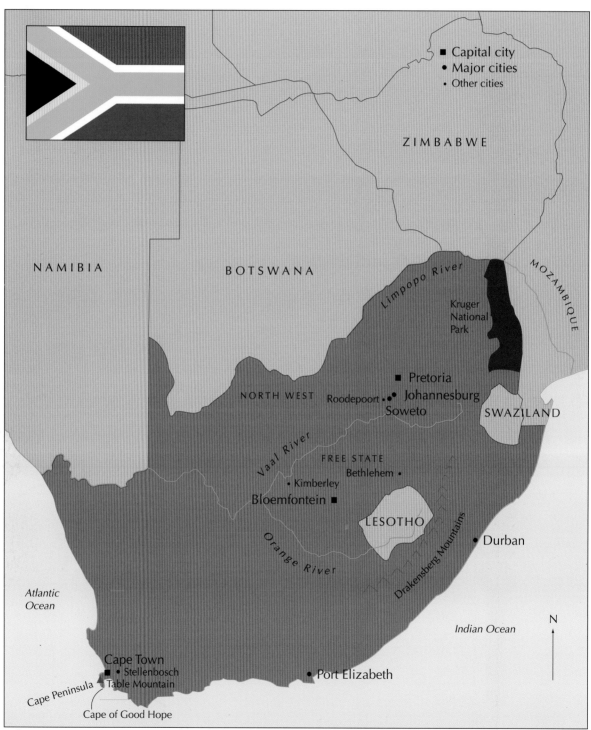

ZIMBABWE

NAMIBIA

BOTSWANA

MOZAMBIQUE

■ Capital city
● Major cities
• Other cities

Limpopo River

Kruger
National
Park

Pretoria ■

Roodepoort • • Johannesburg

NORTH WEST

Soweto

SWAZILAND

Vaal River

FREE STATE

Bethlehem •

• Kimberley

Bloemfontein ■

LESOTHO

Drakensberg Mountains

• Durban

Orange River

Atlantic
Ocean

Indian Ocean

N

Cape Town

■ • Stellenbosch
Table Mountain

Cape Peninsula

Cape of Good Hope

• Port Elizabeth

Welcome to South Africa!

Molweni! My name is Fortune and I come from Cape Town, on the southwestern coast of South Africa.

My country is on the southern tip of the African continent. The Indian Ocean is to the east, and the Atlantic Ocean to the west. Our land has nine provinces, or regions. Our nearest neighbors are Namibia, Botswana, Zimbabwe, Mozambique and Swaziland. The Kingdom of Lesotho is actually *inside* our country!

For many years, South Africa was ruled by a **minority** of white people. This system was known as **apartheid**, which means 'separateness'. Under this system, 80 percent of South Africa's people were forced to live on 13 percent of the land. This land, known as the '**homelands**', was in the poorest parts of the country. In 1993, the black population finally won the same rights as the white population. The days of apartheid were officially over.

Since then, we have seen major changes in our country. Improvements have been made to hospitals, schools, factories, farming and to everyday life. However, we still have a long way to go before all our people can enjoy the same quality of life.

South Africa has 11 official languages including English, **Afrikaans**, Zulu and Xhosa. My family speaks Xhosa and English.

That's me in front!

Family life

My family and I live in Langa. It is one of the many **townships** in Cape Flats. Townships grew up on the edges of major towns, because black people working in the towns needed somewhere to live. They were not allowed to live in 'white family areas' inside the towns. For many years, it was against the law for black people to live even in the townships. People are free to live wherever they like now, but most people cannot afford to move to a better area.

My family is from the Xhosa tribe. My mother, Nobantu, works as a maid for a rich white family in Cape Town. She lives in a small apartment at their house during the week, and comes home on the weekends. My father, Vuziyalo, is a minibus driver. He works long hours.

I have two younger brothers, Knowledge and Lucky, and a younger sister called Winnie. They spend the day at the local creche. Lots of the young children in Langa attend creche while their parents are at work. My grandparents and my aunty live with us. They look after us while my parents are working.

Mealtime at the local creche.

My cousin, Steven, plays outside the spaza. These small, family-run shops sell everyday items such as candles, cold drinks and groceries.

Houses in white areas are modern and comfortable. However, the houses in townships are poorly built. They are often made from old bits of wood and plastic, and from sheets of roofing iron. There is no electricity or running water in most of the township houses.

School

During the years of apartheid, black children and white children went to separate schools. Conditions in schools for black children were very poor. There were not enough classrooms, teachers or books. Many black children left school unable to read or write. These days, the government is making sure that all South African children get a good education. Everyone is encouraged to go to school for at least 10 years.

Children in South Africa start with two years of pre-primary school. Then they study six standards, one each year, at primary school, and four more at secondary school. After that, some students go on to further study at a university or technical college.

My school is close to home. Classes start at 8 a.m. and finish at 2 p.m. We begin the school day by singing a hymn and listening to a Bible reading. My subjects include Xhosa, English, maths, geography, science and history. On Friday afternoons, we help the teachers clean the classrooms.

A group of Sotho students visits a Basotho Cultural Village, near Bethlehem in the Free State, to find out more about their traditional culture.

Sports and leisure

For many years, South African sports teams were unable to compete in world sports events. This was because people from other countries did not agree with South Africa's apartheid policy. Our athletes were banned from both the Olympic and Commonwealth Games. Now that things have changed, our sports teams are again competing in international events.

Our favorite sport is soccer. Bafana Bafana is our national team. Most of the players are black. Thousands of people watch their favorite teams play every week. Other popular sports are netball, cricket, rugby, tennis and golf. Many young people belong to boxing or running clubs.

We have a sunny climate. Water sports such as swimming, scuba diving, sailing and rafting are popular with people who live near the coast.

An inter-school soccer competition in Cape Town.

South African culture

The culture of our country is rich and varied. We have a lively arts scene and every city has its own theaters, galleries and concert halls. People from many races and backgrounds have come together to explore the many problems South Africa has faced. They have done this through their art, plays, movies, novels and music. J. M. Coetzee is one of our award-winning novelists. Nadine Gordimer won the Nobel Prize for Literature in 1991.

Dance has always been part of the African lifestyle. Traditional dances were performed as part of the hunt, before battle, and at weddings and initiation ceremonies. Over the last 20 years, modern performances have used movement and dance to tell the story of our people's struggles.

Traditional music is either chanted or played on instruments such as drums, xylophones and reed pipes. European styles of music, such as classical and jazz, are also popular. Bands such as Ladysmith Black Mambazo, Mango Groove and the Soweto String Quartet, blend traditional and European styles with great success.

Street musicians play in the Basotho Cultural Village.

African masks for sale at a craft market. Traditionally, men carved things from wood and made baskets from grass, while women worked with clay and beads.

Our first paintings were created in the **Stone Age**. Rock artists decorated the walls of their caves with pictures of animals and hunters. Over 3,000 examples of rock art from different ages have been found across the country. Traditional crafts include woodwork, pottery, mat-making, beadwork and basketwork.

Zulu dancers perform a battle dance.

Festivals and religion

Most of our population, about 85 percent, is Christian. Many white people belong to one of the three branches of the Dutch Reformed Church. The church's beginnings can be traced back to the 1600s, when Dutch settlers arrived in South Africa.

Although most black people are Christian, some villagers still follow their tribal beliefs. The **witch doctor** is one of the most important people in the tribe. They have magic powers that allow them to tell the future, or to cure sick people with potions made from dried leaves and bark. Witch doctors call on the spirits of their **ancestors** to help them make decisions. They also believe in mythical creatures such as the *thikoloshe*. This is a hairy, wicked dwarf that loves to play pranks.

We have many festivals that celebrate our culture. People dress in traditional costume, and dance and sing. Every two years, the city of Roodepoort holds an international **eisteddfod**. Choirs and troupes of dancers compete in the festival. People come from all over South Africa to participate in the Grahamstown Festival. They perform opera, play music, and dance in front of the huge audiences.

Gospel singers preach the word to the people in the streets. Most people in South Africa are Christian.

A Dutch Reformed Church in Stellenbosch. South Africa also has mosques, synagogues and Hindu temples.

The Day of the Vow is a Zulu festival. It is held in honor of the 3,000 Zulu warriors who were defeated in battle by the Boers, in the early days of white settlement. Republic Day is celebrated by white people each May. It marks the day, in 1960, that people voted to make the country a **republic**, rather than a **monarchy**.

South African festivals and holidays

New Year's Day	January 1
Human Rights Day	March 21
Easter	March/April
Freedom Day	April 27
Republic Day	May 31
National Arts Festival	July
Kruger Day	October 10
Day of Reconciliation	December 16
Christmas Day	December 25

Food and shopping

We have many different styles of cooking in South Africa. People from our Asian community cook spicy dishes and curries. One of the most popular Indian dishes is called 'bunny chow'. To make it, you slice a loaf of bread in half, tear out the middle, then fill it with curry. Residents with English backgrounds love roast beef, and fish and chips. Some dishes, like kebabs, *bobotie*, and a spicy chutney made from tropical fruit, are a mixture of Asian and European food.

Afrikaners love cooking food outside on a *braai*, or barbecue. Spicy sausages, called *boerewors*, are a favorite barbecue meal. Another popular Afrikaner food is *biltong*. It is made from chewy strips of spicy beef that have been dried in the sun.

Most black South Africans eat simple food. Our main meal is a dish called *mealie*. This is ground maize that has been mixed with water to make a porridge. We eat it plain for breakfast and lunch, and with stewed meat for dinner.

In the cities and larger towns, people buy their goods from shops and supermarkets. In the smaller towns and villages, we shop at markets or at *spazas*. You can buy just about anything you want in a market, from fruits such as mangoes and oranges, to chickens and goats. In the coastal towns, you can also buy freshly caught fish and shellfish.

A local 'B & B', or 'buy and braai'. People choose the cut of meat they want from the butcher's stall. Then they take it next door and cook it themselves on the braai.

Make bobotie

Spicy *bobotie* is one of our most popular dishes. It is an old Malay recipe.

Ask an adult to help you prepare this dish.

You will need:

- 3 slices bread
- 450 milliliters (1 1/2 cup) milk
- 1 large onion, chopped
- 1 tablespoon olive oil
- 500 grams (1 lb) minced beef
- 1 1/2 tablespoons curry powder
- 2 tablespoons lemon juice
- 1/3 cup flaked almonds
- 1/2 cup raisins
- 2 eggs
- pinch of salt and pepper
- a baking dish

What to do:

1 Cut the crusts from the bread. Break the remaining bread into chunks, then soak them in half of the milk. Squeeze the milk out of the bread chunks and set the bread aside.

2 Fry the onion over low heat for 10 minutes.

3 Add the minced beef and fry until well browned.

4 Add the soaked bread chunks, curry powder, lemon juice, nuts, raisins, salt and pepper. Fry for another two minutes, then spoon the mixture into a baking dish.

5 Beat the eggs with the rest of the milk. Pour this mixture over the meat in the baking dish.

6 Bake the *bobotie* in the oven for 1 1/4 hours at 180°C (350°F).

7 Serve with rice mixed with raisins.

Make a lion mask

The lion is the 'king of the beasts'! You can see lions in our many national parks.

You will need:

- a large paper plate
- a pencil
- scissors
- yellow paint
- a paintbrush
- yellow and orange raffia or wool
- tape
- a thick, black marker pen
- a stick

What to do:

1 Hold the plate in front of your face. Ask a friend to gently mark where your eyes are. Draw eyeholes and cut them out.

2 Paint the back of the plate yellow. This will be the lion's face.

3 Cut the raffia or wool into 5 cm (2 inch) lengths. Using small pieces of tape, stick the lengths to the unpainted edge of the mask. This will be the mane.

4 Draw a nose and mouth on your mask. Outline the eye holes with the black pen.

5 Tape a stick to the unpainted side of the mask.

6 Practice your roar!

Landscape and climate

South Africa is a land of contrasts. We have huge mountain ranges, white sandy beaches, rich farmlands, arid deserts, thick forests and rolling grasslands. Our country can be divided into four main regions: grassy **plains**, the Great **Escarpment**, desert regions and coastal plains.

The coastal plains are very narrow. Beyond them are the steep mountain ranges of the Great Escarpment. Their highest peaks are the Drakensburg Mountains. Their name means 'dragon's teeth'. The Zulus have another name for the mountains, which means 'battlement of spears'.

Further inland is the 'veld'. Its name comes from a Dutch word meaning 'field'. This huge, grass plain is about 1,800 meters (5,900 feet) above sea level. Most of our farms and national parks are found in this area. The western part of the country is mainly desert.

South Africa has many steep mountain ranges.

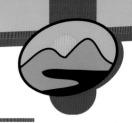

The climate in the coastal regions is warm and sunny. Perfect for swimming!

Our major rivers are the Orange, the Vaal and the Limpopo. The Orange River flows west from the mountains of Lesotho to the Atlantic Ocean at Alexander Bay. South Africa has a low rainfall, so most of our rivers are dry for much of the year.

Grasslands are found in the many dry regions of South Africa.

The weather in South Africa is as varied as our landscape. The east gets plenty of rain. Sometimes it has destructive tropical **cyclones** and **tornadoes**. The northern regions have hot summers and clear, dry winters. Droughts are common in the west.

Temperature and rainfall

	Average daily temperatures		Average annual rainfall
	January	July	
Johannesburg	18°C/64°F	10°C/50°F	750 mm/29.5 in
Durban	24°C/75°F	18°C/64°F	1,000 mm/39 in

Plants and animals

South Africa is famous for having the 'greatest wildlife show on earth'! We have 160 kinds of snakes, 900 species of birds, and 5,000 types of spiders. There are more kinds of mammals here than on any other continent. People come from all over the world to see our amazing range of animals. Lions, leopards, elephants, giraffes, zebras, hyenas, hippopotamuses and antelope all live in the wild here.

National parks and wildlife reserves, such as the Kruger National Park, have been created to help protect our **endangered** animals and plants. Six nations in southern Africa are working on plans to create enormous 'peace parks'. Such parks will allow animals to safely follow their traditional trails. Breeding programs have helped to save rare animals from **extinction**. These include the black rhinoceros, the white square-lipped rhinoceros and the black wildebeest.

A herd of elephants cools down in the mud at a watering hole.

In the dry western regions of South Africa, the only plants that grow are grass and scrub. Jackals, bat-eared foxes and ostriches live in desert regions. In the coastal areas, where rainfall is higher, there are tropical palm trees and forests of yellow-wood, ironwood and cedar trees. These forests attract colorful birds and monkeys. The Cape Floral Kingdom on the Cape Peninsula has 8,500 species of flowers. Six thousand of these are unique to South Africa.

Lions live in groups called prides. Male lions leave most of the hunting to the female lions, but they expect to eat first!

South Africa has:

- the world's largest land mammal (the African elephant)
- the world's smallest land mammal (a shrew the size of a fingertip)
- the world's tallest creature (the giraffe)
- the world's fastest mammal (the cheetah)
- the world's largest reptile (the leatherback turtle)
- the world's largest bird (the ostrich)
- the world's heaviest flying bird (the Kori bustard)

Cities and landmarks

Over half of our population lives in towns and cities such as Cape Town, Johannesburg, Durban and Port Elizabeth. For many years under the laws of apartheid, our towns were divided. There were 'high-income' areas for whites, and 'low-income' areas for blacks. Black people were only allowed into the white areas if they had a special pass. Such a pass was hard to get.

Johannesburg is our largest city. It has a mix of old and new buildings. There are huge shopping malls, office towers, museums and art galleries. Two million people live in Soweto, which is a collection of townships on the outskirts of Johannesburg.

Where people live

- Country areas
- Small towns (less than 50,000 people)
- Cities/towns (between 50,000 and 500,000 people)
- Large cities (more than 500,000 people)

The Twelve Apostles at Camps Bay, on the Cape Peninsula. The Peninsula is famous for its white sandy beaches, seals, birds and wild flowers.

High-income areas had all the modern office buildings, department stores and quality brick housing. The black areas, however, consisted of home-built shacks and shops set up in empty shipping containers. Although these laws have been changed, most black people still live in slums on the edges of cities.

A cable car takes visitors to the top of Table Mountain. This mountain overlooks Cape Town, which is one of the most beautiful cities in the world. Its history dates back to 1652, when it was settled by Dutch traders who supplied food to the ships of the Dutch East India Company.

Industry and agriculture

South Africa is the most **industrialized** nation on the African continent. Our largest industry is mining. We produce more gold than any other country. Diamonds were discovered in the Kimberley region in 1867. The Kimberley diamond mine is 756 meters (2,480 feet) deep. Thirty million ton of earth were removed to mine just three ton of diamonds. One of our major diamond companies, De Beers, is developing a deep-sea mine off the west coast.

Other major industries include steel, iron, electronics and the manufacturing of products such as computers, clothes, ships, trains and cars. Ford, Mitsubishi and Mazda all have factories in Pretoria. Robots do most of the work in them!

Much of our country is covered by steep mountains, so only 13 percent of our land can be farmed. There are two types of farming in South Africa. Commercial farms grow crops, such as maize and tobacco, to sell. Some of these crops are also sold to other countries. Flowers and pot plants are sent to Europe. Our tropical fruit and our wine are famous all over the world.

Many people run their own businesses in the townships. This hair salon has been set up inside an empty shipping container.

Orange orchards near Brits, in the North-West Province.

The other type of farming is called subsistence farming. People on these farms grow only enough maize and vegetables to feed themselves. There is none left to sell. They may also keep a cow, or some pigs or chickens.

Every year, thousands of tourists visit South Africa. Attractions include our stunning scenery, traditional culture and the wildlife in our national parks. The tourists have helped to create jobs for our people. They work as tour guides, **game wardens**, waiters and taxi-drivers.

The Groot Constantia vineyard, on the Cape Peninsula. Wine and brandy are two of South Africa's main exports.

25

Transportation

South Africa has the best transportation system on the African continent. A government-owned company, Transnet, looks after six major areas of transportation. These include the railways, roads, ports and airlines.

Highways link all our major cities, and connect us to neighboring countries such as Zimbabwe and Mozambique. There are nine major airports in South Africa. Our international airports are in Cape Town, Johannesburg and Durban. Our largest airline is South African Airways, or SAA.

Because most South Africans are unable to afford cars, our rail service is very important. Many people from the townships travel to work by train. Trains also transport materials such as coal, iron ore and cement. During the days of apartheid, there were separate carriages for black and white people. Now people can sit wherever they like.

The Blue Train is a famous luxury passenger train that runs from Johannesburg to Cape Town. It snakes through the mountains, giving passengers wonderful views of our mountain scenery.

Minibuses, which are small commercial vans, are a popular way of travelling around cities.

Durban Port, in Natal Bay, handles heavy cargo such as iron ore and steel.

People usually walk or take minibus taxis when travelling within the townships. Minibuses are also used for longer journeys. They are cheap and fast, but sometimes they are dangerous to travel in. The drivers cram in as many people as they can, and often drive too fast. On the weekends, the roads are full of minibuses. They bring back people from their jobs in the cities to their homes in the townships.

Donkey carts can still be seen in country areas.

History and government

The first people to live in the south of Africa were members of the San and Khoikhoi tribes. Other tribes moved down from the north in the 1400s and 1500s. They pushed the San and Khoikhoi people to the desert areas in the west.

Europeans first arrived in 1488. The Portuguese sailor Bartolemeu Diaz was the first white man to visit the Cape of Good Hope. In the 1600s, the Dutch East India Company set up a settlement at the Cape to provide supplies for their ships. By the late 1700s, over 15,000 Dutch settlers were living in southern Africa. They were called Boers, which means 'farmers' in Dutch.

British settlers began to arrive in the early 1800s. This prompted the Dutch to make their 'Great Trek' further inland. They wanted to escape British rule and to find new land of their own. When gold and diamonds were discovered, war broke out between the British and Dutch settlers over who should control the mines. Black people went to work in the mines. Later, workers from India and China joined them, establishing the Asian community in South Africa.

A Zulu village chief. Zulus and other tribes lived in southern Africa for many centuries before white settlers arrived.

A mural of Nelson Mandela in Soweto. He became the first black president of South Africa. Mandela spent 27 years in jail because he believed that black people and white people were equals.

From the 1820s until 1994, South Africa was ruled by white people. They came from either Dutch or British backgrounds. Black people were treated unfairly by the white people. However, they were unable to change things because they had no right to vote. In the 1950s, the government introduced apartheid. Black people were forced to live in homelands, which were in the poorest parts of the South African countryside. They were not allowed to sit next to white people on buses or trains, to eat in the same restaurants, or go to the same schools as whites. They could only live near a town if they had a job in that town.

During the 1970s and 1980s, black people began to rebel against the white government. Nelson Mandela played an important role in changing things for the better. He was a member of the **African National Congress**, or ANC. After four years of talks, all South Africans were finally allowed to vote in 1994. Nelson Mandela became the new president. Apartheid was finally over. However, it left behind many problems for the people of South Africa, both black and white.

Fact file

Official name Republic of South Africa		**Population** 44,400,000	**Land area** 1,219,090 square kilometers (475,445 square miles)

Government republic	**Languages** 11 official languages, including Afrikaans, English, Xhosa, Zulu, Ndebele, Swazi		**Religion** Christianity, traditional African religions, Islam, Hinduism
Currency Rand (R) R1 = 100 cents		**Capital cities** Pretoria (administrative), Cape Town (legislative), Bloemfontein (judicial)	**Major cities** Johannesburg, Durban, Port Elizabeth
		**Climate** dry inland with sunny days and cool nights, hot and humid on the east coast	
Major rivers Orange, Vaal, Limpopo		**Length of coastline** 2,798 kilometers (1,739 miles)	**Highest mountain range** Drakensburg Mountains
Main farm products corn, wheat, sugarcane, fruit, vegetables, beef, poultry, mutton, wool, dairy products	**Main industries** mining, tourism, steel, iron, electronics, manufacturing (clothes, ships, trains and cars)		**Natural resources** gold, chromium, coal, iron ore, manganese, nickel, diamonds, salt, natural gas

Glossary

African National Congress	a political party that has campaigned for equal rights for black people since 1912, even after it was banned by the white government
Afrikaans	The language spoken by Afrikaners
Afrikaners	white South Africans who are descended from the original Dutch settlers
ancestors	family members who came before you
apartheid	the former government policy of 'separateness' that kept black people apart from whites, and deprived them of basic rights
cyclones	dangerous tropical storms with high winds and heavy rain
eisteddfod	a competition for dance, music and drama
endangered	refers to an animal or plant species that is at risk of dying out
escarpment	a steep bank
extinction	when no more animals of this kind are left on earth
game wardens	people who look after wild animals in a national park
homelands	areas that were set aside by the white government for black people to live in; they were usually far from white towns
industrialized	describes a country which uses machinery for making products and for farming
minority	a smaller number or smaller part
monarchy	a country that is ruled by a king, queen or emperor
plains	large areas of flat land
republic	a country that is ruled by an elected leader
Stone Age	a time in the past when people used tools made of stone
tornadoes	violent whirlwinds that move across the land causing destruction
townships	separate areas for non-white people on the edges of white towns
witch doctor	an important member of a tribe who heals people using traditional methods

Index

English	Afrikaans	Xhosa
one	*een*	*isinye*
two	*twee*	*isibini*
three	*drie*	*isithathu*
four	*vier*	*isine*
five	*vyf*	*isihianu*
six	*ses*	*isithandathu*
seven	*sewe*	*isixhenxe*
eight	*agt*	*isibhozo*
nine	*nege*	*ithoba*
ten	*tien*	*ishumi*

Afrikaans
Xhosa
English

molweni
hallo
hello

goodbye
sala kakuhle
totsiens

enkosi
thank you
dankie